To:

_____

From:

_____

Date:

_____

GodMoments
for
Men

Andrew Holmes

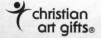

GodMoments for Men

Developed in co-operation with Educational Publishing Concepts

© 2012 Christian Art Gifts, RSA
        Christian Art Gifts Inc., IL, USA

Designed by Christian Art Gifts

Images used under license from Shutterstock.com

Unless otherwise indicated, Scripture quotations are taken from
the *Holy Bible,* New International Version® NIV®. Copyright © 1973,
1978, 1984, 2011 by International Bible Society. Used by permission of
Zondervan Publishing House. All rights reserved.

Scripture quotations marked NLT are taken from the *Holy Bible,* New
Living Translation®, second edition. Copyright © 1996, 2004 by Tyndale
House Publishers, Inc., Carol Stream, Illinois 60188. All rights reserved.

Scripture quotations marked ESV are taken from the *Holy Bible,* English
Standard Version. Copyright © 2001 by Crossway Bibles, a division of
Good News Publishers. Used by permission. All rights reserved.

Scripture quotations marked MSG are taken from THE MESSAGE. Copyright
© by Eugene H. Peterson, 1993, 1994, 1995, 1996, 2000, 2001, 2002 by
NavPress Publishing Group. Used by permission.

Scripture quotations marked NCV are taken from the *Holy Bible,*
New Century Version®. Copyright © 1987, 1988, 1991, 2005 by Word
Publishing, a division of Thomas Nelson, Inc. Used by permission.

Printed in China

ISBN 978-1-77036-906-1

12 13 14 15 16 17 18 19 20 21 – 12 11 10 9 8 7 6 5 4 3

Introduction

A word of caution

A book like this is an interesting purchase for a man. It isn't a how-to book. You're not going to find within its pages the secret to doubling your income or snagging that promotion.

This book isn't a spy novel or sports biography or political memoir either. There are no car chases or bloody battle scenes.

What exactly is this book? It's an on-ramp. It's that short jot between the auxiliary road we all start our day on and the furious freeway we spend the rest of it navigating.

The caution? Asphalt on-ramps require great speed to make the transition successful. The on-ramp to our heart bids us to slow down, focus on and commit to a perspective. If we will give God a moment, He'll give us manna.

Beginning

"Blessed is the man who perseveres under trial, because when he has stood the test, he will receive the crown of life that God has promised to those who love Him."

JAMES 1:12

Disappointment, disillusionment, despair. These are common experiences. Just part of life, right? Sure. But look closer and you'll likely find a link between what you thought should or would be and what, in fact, is. Challenge yourself to see what comes your way as your way to become. Did you catch that?

The reality is God has begun a very good work in you and He is headstrong to complete it. Embrace that reality.

Happiness may look entirely different from the way you imagine it.

BYRON KATIE

Knowing God

Oh, the depth of the riches and wisdom and knowledge of God! How unsearchable are His judgments and how inscrutable His ways. "For who has known the mind of the Lord, or who has been His counselor?"

Romans 11:33-34 esv

Sometimes it's hard to love God. Sometimes it's hard to see God as fair or truly kind or merciful. One minute God "doesn't want anyone to perish" and the next minute He is ready to "spew someone out of His mouth."

Is it possible these types of internal struggles spring forth from the same misguided assumption intellectual atheists argue from: a dangerously high opinion of our opinions?

It's humbling enough to admit we don't have all the answers but what do we do when we finally come to the realization that we don't even know how to ask the right questions? I think I know the answer to the latter. We fall on our faces and join our wise brother Job in saying, "I'm shutting up now, Lord."

God is not fractured, but we are, and so we develop a fractured view of God.

Rabbi Russell Resnik

Focus

If only for this life we have hope in Christ,
we are to be pitied more than all men.

1 CORINTHIANS 15:19

I remember a song from Christian radio during the seventies. The hook was an old saying, if we're too heavenly-minded, we'll be no earthly good. I liked the song a lot and I think the writer did a good job of narrowing the application of the saying but I have to admit I've never been guilty of having my thoughts so focused on heaven that I've neglected earth. I have the opposite problem! And I don't think I'm alone.

Jesus warned us that the cares, worries and desires of this life easily choke out passion for the things of God and my life illustrates this all too well. We must follow Paul's admonition to "set our minds on things above" or we'll undo our faith and diminish our impact on our world.

Holding on is easier when we are excited about where we're headed. Heed Jesus' promise to return and take us to that wonderful place He's been preparing. Then, like the beautiful hymn says, "the things of earth will grow strangely dim in the light of His glory and grace."

If you read history you will find that the
Christians who did most for the present world
were precisely those who thought most of the next.

C. S. LEWIS

Perspective

*But one thing I do: Forgetting what is
behind and straining toward what is ahead,
I press on toward the goal to win the prize for
which God has called me heavenward in Christ Jesus.*

PHILIPPIANS 3:13-14

Past failures can leave you feeling like Humpty Dumpty. When the regrets of yesterday circle the wagons around your mind, it's easy to embrace the lie that "all the king's horses and all the king's men" simply can't put it all back together again.

Of course, feelings are far from fact. And yet, unless we're vigilant, those dark feelings stealthily become the basis for beliefs – beliefs that lead to actions that invite never-ending waves of real-life consequences.

The solution is in the perspective.

*I missed over 9, 000 shots in my career.
I've lost over 300 games ... I've failed over and
over in my life. And that is why I succeed.*

MICHAEL JORDAN

Trusting

Blessed is the man who trusts in the Lord,
whose confidence is in Him.
JEREMIAH 17:7

I'll believe it when I see it with my own eyes. If I have to see it with my own eyes, then there is no believing involved. Trust consists of not having to see it with any eyes, but rather with a feeling in the heart and mind that everything is going to be alright, even if there is no concrete proof.

We've become a nation of "proof-wanters" for almost everything in our lives. New products have to prove it can get the stain out. Juries have to get proof beyond a reasonable doubt. Scientists have to prove theories. We don't seem to trust anyone or in much of anything anymore, much less trust in an all-powerful being.

Over two hundred years ago, our founding fathers still trusted in things that can't necessarily be seen. It says so on our money. I look around and see so many wonderful things that can only be explained by God's generosity and desire to take care of me. I trust Him. He's done a good job so far.

All I have seen teaches me to trust the
Creator for all I have not seen.
RALPH WALDO EMERSON

The Little Things

*If you are faithful in little things, you will be faithful
in large ones. But if you are dishonest in little things,
you won't be honest with greater responsibilities.*

LUKE 16:10 NLT

I always try to impress others with something
spectacular or amazing because I want them to take
notice, feeling that unless it's a real feast for the eyes
or way above what is expected, then it's not of much
significance and will be disappointing.

I don't know why I feel this way because I always
notice the little things that people do for me that are
unassuming and simple.

When my kids clean up a mess they made in the
kitchen or wash some of my clothes when they are doing
their own laundry, I notice it and feel happy and grateful
that I instilled a giving spirit in them.

My wife realized how frustrating my day had been
and gave me a back massage while listening to my
complaints about work. It was a little thing that made
me feel better physically and emotionally. It meant a lot
to me.

Little things add up and make life better for those on
the receiving end, as well as on the giving end.

*Everyone is trying to accomplish something big,
not realizing that life is made up of little things.*

FRANK A. CLARK

Changed Heart

As Jesus was getting back into the boat, the man who was freed from the demons begged to go with Him. But Jesus would not let him. He said, "Go home to your family and tell them how much the Lord has done for you and how He has had mercy on you."

MARK 5:18 NCV

Who hasn't secretly wished for one good rub on Aladdin's lamp or one mighty swish of a magic wand? The desire to instantly receive something we want but the dread of putting in the time to receive can be powerful – especially on the heels of genuine repentance and change.

Actions have consequences, even – no, particularly – for the devout, for those seeking to follow the Savior. Most often, God changes your heart – not your world.

That, my brother, is your mission, a changed heart, starting with the one you may have wrecked.

You can't believe yourself out of something you behaved yourself into.

DR. KELVIN J. KELLEY

Love More

"Love your enemies, do good to them,
and lend to them without hoping to get anything back.
Then you will have a great reward, and you will be
children of the Most High God, because He is kind
even to people who are ungrateful and full of sin."

LUKE 6:35 NCV

Certainly Paul's admonition to "make every effort to live at peace with everyone" is to be followed zealously. Still, conflicts will occur – sometimes severe ones. A quick glance at Paul's own life attests to this fact. Not to mention our Lord's.

Doing good won't make everything in your life great. Paradoxically, sometimes it will do the opposite. Didn't Christ Himself tell us to expect this? "Just as the world hated Me," He told us, "It will hate you."

What do we do in response? The same thing Jesus did. Love more.

You have enemies? Good. That means you've
stood up for something, sometime in your life.
WINSTON CHURCHILL

Surrender

Don't become so well-adjusted to your culture that you fit into it without even thinking. Instead, fix your attention on God. You'll be changed from the inside out. Readily recognize what He wants from you, and quickly respond to it. Unlike the culture around you, always dragging you down to its level of immaturity, God brings the best out of you, develops well-formed maturity in you.

ROMANS 12:2 MSG

A big movement in recent years asserts that Christianity as practiced today – like in our society at large – has "sissified" men.

Because of this, they say, men are, understandably (even genetically), losing interest in the things of God. Maybe they're right. Still, I can't help but feel a bit cautious.

Maybe the church has spent too much time on the gentle side of Jesus. Then again, maybe not. Maybe the real transformation comes at the point of full surrender – including the courageous abandonment of all those "manly" dispositions I so ruggedly cling to.

You seek the heights of manhood when you seek the depths of God.

EDWIN LOUIS COLE

Warning Sign

Pride goes before destruction,
a haughty spirit before a fall.
PROVERBS 16:18

I've had the ego-stroking experience of signing an autograph or two (OK, it was two. And they were for my daughter). But even the adoration of a three-year-old can go to your head if you let it. Maybe not in a red carpet kind of way but in a "I really am pretty cool" kind of way.

Pride, we're cautioned, goes before a fall. Not "sometimes" or "most times" or "every now and then." The Word is teaching us about a sequence that nature is powerless to sever. Pride is a predictor, like a "set" in volleyball. It screams: "A 'spike' is on its way!"

Heed its warning or find yourself face-flat on the floor.

It strikes me as unfair, and even in bad taste, to select
a few of them for boundless admiration, attributing
superhuman powers of mind and character to them.
ALBERT EINSTEIN

What's Done Is Done

Rather, it should be that of your inner self,
the unfading beauty of a gentle and quiet spirit,
which is of great worth in God's sight.
1 PETER 3:4

Worrying about what I've done is useless because it's already done. Fretting over what is before me only makes me anxious and the situation more stressful than it need be. What I should be focusing on is what's inside me. That's what makes me who I am and how I handle life.

What's in my heart and spirit is the driving force behind how I treat others and what kind of example I am for Christ.

When I see how much I dwell on my past mistakes, instead of zoning in on having a loving attitude and an open hand to all of God's children, I get a queasy feeling in the pit of my stomach, because I usually know when I'm not doing what I should be doing.

Like too many people, I just don't always make the right choice. Once I get my heart right with God, I keep my eyes on Jesus and see all the wonderful joys of being alive.

What lies behind us and what lies ahead of us
are tiny matters compared to what lies within us.
HENRY STANLEY HASKINS

Giving In

Watch and pray so that you will not fall into temptation.
The spirit is willing, but the body is weak.
MATTHEW 26:41

Temptation taunts and tantalizes my total being at every turn. It pulls at my wants and desires, trying to convince me that submitting just a little will be in my best interests. Besides, everybody's doing it, has it already, or will be getting it soon. I don't want to be left out.

I walk into a store and immediately my mind is spinning with thoughts of "I'd really love to have that." I sit down in my favorite restaurant and say, "Now, what do I want tonight?" I'm glued to the TV, almost chanting in unison with the commercial, "Wouldn't I look great driving that new car!"

I hardly ever simply fill my needs because I'm so busy giving in to my wants. I tell myself that I don't really need it, that I need to save the money and put it to better use. Yet I notice that I really enjoy the dance with temptation, and when I do persevere and stay on the straight and narrow for a while, I long for a new temptation to come along and swing me around the dance floor one more time. Ask God to help you resist temptation.

Most people want to be delivered from temptation
but would like it to keep in touch.
ROBERT ORBEN

The High Road

*Do not repay evil for evil or reviling for reviling,
but on the contrary, bless, for to this you were called,
that you may obtain a blessing.*
1 PETER 3:9 ESV

Booker T. Washington accomplished a great deal in his brief 59 years on this earth. Born just nine years before the Emancipation, he spent the entirety of his life teaching fellow blacks to live self-reliant lives – and making enemies on both sides as he did. Many blacks reviled him for being "too accommodating to the white man."

Of his long list of truly impressive achievements, one dwarfs them all: he didn't hate back. That's monumental! Booker T. Washington understood that hating others is the surest way to diminish yourself. Hating others shrinks you. It reduces your capacity to express the life God calls you to live. In his words, it "narrows and degrades" your own soul. He's right.

Do God's good today and if someone reviles you because of it, don't hate him. Pray that his heart will grow.

*I will permit no man to narrow and
degrade my soul by making me hate him.*
BOOKER T. WASHINGTON

Envy

Peace of mind means a healthy body,
but jealousy will rot your bones.
PROVERBS 14:30 NCV

The story goes there were two men sharing a hospital room divided by a curtain. The man by the window would tell his roommate what he saw happening in the park below. He told of the parade, enthusiastically describing every detail. He told of family reunions and of a nervous soldier's marriage proposal.

His play-by-play descriptions became like balm to the roommate's soul. Until this thought slithered its way into the roommate's heart: Why does he get the bed by the window? Devoured by the thought, envy turned to bitterness, bitterness to resentment, resentment to hatred. No more stories. No more friendship. No more joy.

After the man died, the roommate demanded the bed by the window only to find it faced a brick wall.

Envy is the ulcer of the soul.
SOCRATES

Belief and Faith

*What good is it, my brothers and sisters, if someone claims
to have faith but has no deeds? Can such faith save them?
Suppose a brother or a sister is without clothes
and daily food. If one of you says to them, "Go in peace;
keep warm and well fed," but does nothing about their
physical needs, what good is it? In the same way, faith by
itself, if it is not accompanied by action, is dead.*

JAMES 2:14-17

Faith is action. Faith moves. It isn't neutral or non-committal. Many use belief and faith interchangeably but that isn't a true exchange at all. Faith and belief, while often connected, are far from being synonymous.

We can believe something and yet remain unengaged regarding that belief. Not so with faith. Faith is engagement. Faith doesn't become faith via expression – faith is expression. Belief can watch from the bleachers. Faith is in the game.

Ready for a tough question? It's important to ask: Do I merely believe in the truth Christ exampled and taught, or, am I defined by my faith in Him? And if, like me, you're a gurgling mix of both: Am I willing to go deeper till His heart fully infuses my own?

*Faith is the daring of the soul to
go farther than it can see.*

WILLIAM NEWTON CLARKE

Discipline

My child, don't reject the Lord's discipline, and don't be upset when He corrects you. For the Lord corrects those He loves, just as a father corrects a child in whom He delights.

PROVERBS 3:11-12 NLT

"This will be the whipping of your life, son." And it was. I was ten years old and had just deliberately disobeyed my daddy's clear instruction. I had asked him if I could walk to the nearby store. He said, "No, we're about to leave for church." But I had two dollars burning a hole in my pocket and had made up my mind to buy myself some candy. So off I went.

Two things are certain: my daddy loved me very much; and, no candy is worth what I paid for it. Did I enjoy the correction? Uh, no. Did I benefit from it? No doubt about it.

Good daddies beat good candy any day of the week because the sweetness of a loving father's discipline lasts a lifetime.

Corn is cleaned with wind,
and the soul with chastening.
GEORGE HERBERT

Be Enthusiastic

"I know the plans I have for you," declares the Lord,
"plans to prosper you and not to harm you,
plans to give you hope and a future."
Jeremiah 29:11

It seems really weird to me that when I used to look at my parents when they were my current age, I couldn't fathom how old they were. They seemed really old, but now that I'm 53, it doesn't seem so old. I don't feel old. Sure, I see some looser skin, some spots on my arms, wrinkles around the eyes, definitely a lot less hair, and aches and pains that let me know I'm no spring chicken anymore, but I don't feel old, maybe because I do have enthusiasm in my life.

I have enthusiasm for my family, being a teacher, my new granddaughter, being with fellow Christians, and many other things that God sends my way. Of course, everything He sends my way isn't always fun or exciting, sometimes downright annoying.

But taking these little traumas and making them bearable shows the strength that Christ has when I let Him lead the way. I'll admit, there are times when I try to do it alone. But I can't, because even when I think I'm alone, He's there with me, now and forever.

Years wrinkle the skin, but to give up
enthusiasm wrinkles the soul.
Samuel Ullman

Stick with the Plan

We also rejoice in our sufferings, because
we know that suffering produces perseverance;
perseverance, character; and character, hope.

ROMANS 5:3-4

The ability to stay with one thing and see it through is not a trait that everyone has. I know that I have a tough time sticking to something when the going gets tough. Too often I give up because I'm frustrated with the situation or tired of not reaching my goal. It's so much easier to give up than to go through the hardships and struggles that come my way.

I bought a rolling kitchen island that had to be assembled. You know the kind that comes with confusing instructions and ten thousand little parts, and invariably, has a few parts missing.

About halfway through the project, I became very frustrated because nothing fitted correctly and the instructions were extremely vague. I felt like sticking it back in the box and returning it to the store. But I tarried on, and several hours later had a fairly nice island that we've enjoyed on a daily basis.

Sometimes we have to drive down rough roads filled with many potholes in order to arrive at our final destination, making the journey worthwhile.

Consider the postage stamp: its usefulness consists
in the ability to stick to one thing till it gets there.

JOSH BILLINGS

Hope

"When these things begin to take place, stand up and lift up your heads, because your redemption is drawing near."
LUKE 21:28

Surely you know by now that the first part of the quote below is exhaustingly true. Like tiny invaders eating away at a lush garden, troubles are a daily part of our world. When they begin to nibble our joys away, something inside of us feels violated. Don't they care that they're destroying a sanctuary of beauty? Stare at their destruction and they win. Refocus your eyes on the beauty and you'll be invited back into the vision.

God's Spirit is like that, too. Next time you're curled up at the bottom of the deepest pit of despair, tilt your ear toward heaven. God is forever inviting you back to hope, to dream, to love, to life.

The Divine Artist is calling the artist in you to see afresh the masterpiece He is painting on the canvas of your soul. The best is yet to come.

Life beats down and crushes the soul and art reminds you that you have one.
STELLA ADLER

Your Time

Remember the Sabbath day by keeping it holy.
EXODUS 20:8

A famous bumper sticker once read: "He who dies with the most toys wins." Too intoxicated with materialism to see it for the sobering indictment it was, many proudly pasted it on their Porsches as proof they were leading the pack.

We continue to equate success with prosperity, only we've switched our definition from "toys" to "time." Specifically, leisure time. Down time. Blow-off time. Now we are prosperous when we have stashed enough cash to make a mad dash away.

I'm into taking breaks but I also wonder if taking too many breaks ... breaks me?

I'm wondering if I've contorted God's idea of Sabbath into my infatuation of, well – to put it bluntly, killing time.

Has your idle time become idol time, with you at the center of it? It begs an answer.

My soul is more at rest from the tempter
when I am busily employed.
FRANCIS ASBURY

Ask Direction

Then Jonah prayed to his God from the belly of the fish.
He prayed: "In trouble, deep trouble, I prayed to God.
He answered me. From the belly of the grave I cried,
'Help!' You heard my cry."

JONAH 2:2 MSG

I have a love/hate relationship with the "positive mental attitude" movement. The worship-like obsession of dent-of-will giddiness leaves Grand Canyons of gaps in thinking to me. On the flip side, I love the intentional self-direction. To allow yourself to be engulfed in despair is – in a word – depressing.

Where's God in all this?

In 1 Samuel 30, David and his mighty men find their village destroyed and their wives and kids taken captive. They "wept aloud" (translation: gut-wrenching wailing) to the point of exhaustion, it says. Then, the men talk (translation: froth at the mouth) of stoning David.

Here's the God-part – the God-heart:

BUT DAVID FOUND STRENGTH
IN THE LORD HIS GOD.

Wow. Then David asked God for direction – and got it. Interesting. What could've ended in a bloodbath became a point of breakthrough and restoration.

The world is extremely interesting to a joyful soul.
ALEXANDRA STODDARD

God Is Holy

"I hate your new moon celebrations and your annual
festivals. They are a burden to Me. I cannot stand them!
When you lift up your hands in prayer, I will not look.
Wash yourselves and be clean! Get your sins out of My sight.
Give up your evil ways. Learn to do good."

ISAIAH 1:14-17 NLT

There is a sense of "you scratch my back, I'll scratch yours" when it comes to our view of how relationships work. A "give and take." A "back and forth." Even, at times, a "go along to get along." These have their place in our relationships with one another but what about with God? Is there a similar flexibility of convictions or values when interacting with our Creator?

The concept of true holiness overloads our neurons – the reality of it is beyond our comprehension. And yet that's where God resides. That's His address.

So when we seek to journey with Jesus, we must abandon our sense of equality and embrace God's gracious offer to be lavished upon while being less in return, to be warmly welcomed and still horrifically unworthy.

Save your placations for a dime store messiah. Obedience is birthed in the wholehearted acceptance that God is GOD. Hello?

Prepare thy soul calmly to obey; such offering will be
more acceptable to God than every other sacrifice.

METASTASIO

Make a Difference

*Do not let any unwholesome talk come out of your mouths,
but only what is helpful for building others up according
to their needs, that it may benefit those who listen.*

EPHESIANS 4:29

A few years ago while teaching elementary students, I observed a student who had many behavioral and self-worth issues in the grade below the one I was teaching. Everyone knew he'd be in our grade the next year and all I could keep thinking was "just watch, he'll end up in my class." And he did.

I knew things were going to have to be totally different for this student. I couldn't treat him in the same way I had taught most of the other kids. I thought, "Somehow I'm going to make this work. I'll just love him to death and hope that gives him some self-esteem."

He didn't feel like he fit in with the other students, so I bought him some new clothes and shoes. I took him out to eat and invited him to do some things with my family. I treated him like he mattered.

It made such a difference. He started doing his assignments, was more open to receiving help when he struggled, and began enjoying school instead of dreading it. We can make a difference.

*Treat a person as he is,
and he will remain as he is.
Treat him as he could be,
and he will become what he should be.*

JIMMY JOHNSON

Look Forward

Whatever is true, whatever is honorable, whatever is just, whatever is pure, whatever is lovely, whatever is commendable, if there is any excellence, if there is anything worthy of praise, think about these things.

<small>PHILIPPIANS 4:8 ESV</small>

I can't, never could. Sounds like something one of my teachers said, if not several of them. Putting forth an effort is a real struggle for many people, much less being positive about a good outcome.

At times, I'm right in there, complaining about my failure before I've even started the task, which in turn makes me want to put it off until tomorrow, and it starts to snowball. When I do things that I look forward to doing, I do them so much better.

This leads me to ask, "Why don't I look forward to everything I do?" If I'm looking forward to it, then I'm happy to do it. If I'm happy to do it, I have a much more positive attitude, an attitude that leads me down the road of success.

It's hard to be happy about everything you do because some things are just not that exciting, and some are absolutely boring. But if you're trying to achieve something, you've got to feel that you have a chance.

I never saw a pessimistic general win a battle.

<small>E. E. CUMMINGS</small>

Truth

The Lord is my shepherd, I shall not be in want.
PSALM 23:1

Sticks and stones may break my bones, as the saying goes, but words can never hurt me. Experience – and millions in therapy (or, in need of it!) – show this for what it is: a lie.

Words are the primary method of inflicting pain on another. If only there was a vaccine to make us immune to these hurtful expressions!

There is. It's called "truth." Not temporary truth like "but I really am fat." I'm talking about ultimate truth. The kind of truth Jesus meant when He said "the truth shall set you free." The kind of truth that insulates our fragile frame from fiery darts from the enemy so we can love without looking back and give without need of repayment. The kind of truth that fills us.

What is that truth? It's that God's love is enough. Be satisfied in God's opinion about you.

Whenever anyone has offended me, I try to raise my soul so high that the offense cannot reach it.
RENE DESCARTES

Walking with God

*The Lord directs our steps, so why try to
understand everything along the way?*
PROVERBS 20:24 NLT

Walking in the Spirit is like being a football
running back. There's an overall play to direct you but
the real yardage is gained by dashing through the open
spaces. The Spirit of God shows us those spaces. Some
look like 350 pound obstacles to us – but not to God.
He sees the block coming. Our job is simply to put our
weight into it and go.

This is where we often miss God and find ourselves
stuck in the middle row of religion. Didn't Jesus say, "I
only do what I see My Father doing?" Wasn't it Jesus
who urged His followers to wait for the Holy Spirit who
"will guide you into all things"?

Jesus isn't looking for faithful churchgoers. He's
looking for copycats. He wants folks like you and me
who will simply "do what our Father is doing." Just like
He did.

*It takes imagination to walk with God.
Mostly His, of course. Ours simply determines
the extent to which He can express it.*
ANDY HOLMES

Death

*For to me, living means living for Christ,
and dying is even better.*
PHILIPPIANS 1:21 NLT

I know death isn't the cheeriest of meditational topics but I think, perhaps, it should be. Jesus thought about His death. It was the doorway to the joy set before Him. Stephen saw heaven open up – and it thrilled his soul. Paul tells us death – and what surely follows – is an ideal source of encouragement.

Maybe the best way to live our life today is to live it in clear view of our life in that endless tomorrow. When we boldly embrace the inescapable certainty of death, we'll see sin's fleeting allure in a truer context; its temporary pleasures for the insidious invaders they really are.

Sin is the virus that kills. Death – in Christ – is the atonement that heals.

*The taste of death is upon my lips. I feel
something that is not of this earth.*
MOZART

Keep Swimming

Above all else, guard your heart,
for it is the wellspring of life.
PROVERBS 4:23

How did I end up here? Think back. Way back. Looking at a dirty magazine for the first time. Teenage explorations. Watching late night infomercials in a darkened den. "Call me," they moan. Going out of your way to check out a woman's rear. Internet obsessions. I'm not hurting anyone, you tell yourself. Unconvincingly.

Swim against the current. And, no, the current will not go away. But neither will you drown in it as long as you keep swimming.

No one ever suddenly became depraved.
DECIMUS JUNIUS JUVENALIS

Give Thanks

Be cheerful no matter what; pray all the time;
thank God no matter what happens. This is the way
God wants you who belong to Christ Jesus to live.
1 THESSALONIANS 5:18 MSG

This past weekend I experienced the birth of my first grandchild. It was a tremendous event that chronicled the start of a new generation in my family.

When I saw her precious little face, I knew that I had truly been blessed by God. It took me back to the same time period when the agency brought our daughter to our home, and we laid eyes on her for the first time. Again, another time I was blessed.

It seems that I forget so often just how many times God does bless me and my family. But why does it take special times like these to make me realize what I should know every day?

These are only two of countless blessings that He bestows on me constantly. I don't usually take the time to acknowledge all He has done, except for the typical mentioning in prayers. My heart can tell you immediately when a blessing occurs, but I don't regularly seem to think about it in my head.

The hardest arithmetic to master is that which
enables us to count our blessings.
ERIC HOFFER

Peace in Your Heart

Let the peace of Christ rule in your hearts, since as members of one body you were called to peace. And be thankful.
COLOSSIANS 3:15

I wish we all had the understanding that would bring peace to the world. That would be ideal. But will man ever totally get to that kind of understanding? I mean, if we can't even comprehend the peace God has and emanates into all He does, then how can we possibly expect that understanding that would bring peace to the world?

The thing that I can do something about is being satisfied, happy, content. That is a peace that I can achieve, a peace in my heart and soul that will sustain me until the day I get to see my Lord and Savior, Jesus Christ.

Unfortunately, being content is a constant struggle I face. I'm always wanting something new or feeling that somehow my life could be better. I know I've had moments of peace that touched me deeply throughout my life, like when a child touches my heart, meeting and marrying my wife, helping those less fortunate, or realizing how God blessed me when my wife survived her stroke. That's why I keep striving to feel peace through God.

I do not want the peace that passeth understanding.
I want the understanding which bringeth peace.
HELEN KELLER

No "Free Lunch"

We can rejoice, too, when we run into problems and trials,
for we know that they help us develop endurance.
And endurance develops strength of character,
and character strengthens our confident hope of salvation.
And this hope will not lead to disappointment.

ROMANS 5:3-5 NLT

It's odd how swayed we are by promises of easy living and lottery-like rewards. Familiar with any of these?

Just say "charge it."

"You deserve a break today."

"Double your pleasure. Double your fun."

These are effective slogans from hugely successful products and companies. I get their appeal – and I buy their products as often as you do. I can't help but wonder if a steady diet of easy solutions and stress-free options does us more harm than good.

While we often envy the one who scratches off an instant fortune, we admire the person who perseveres.

Why is that? Because God designed us with a holy hunger to be hardy. So next time life presents you with a challenge, roll up your sleeves and put on another pot of coffee. God has a promotion for you in mind.

Character cannot be developed in ease and quiet. Only through experience of trial and suffering can the soul be strengthened, ambition inspired, and success achieved.

HELEN KELLER

You Are Special

*You show that you are a letter from Christ
sent through us. This letter is not written with ink
but with the Spirit of the living God. It is not
written on stone tablets but on human hearts.*

2 CORINTHIANS 3:3 NCV

Jesse figured he'd more than covered his bases
when he told each of his sons to wash up and put their
best togas on. Samuel arrived, Jesse's boys lined up and
Samuel studied each one.

Much to Samuel's (and, no doubt, Jesse's) surprise,
Eliab was not God's man of the hour. Jesse nudged
Abinadab forward. Nope again. Then Shimea, followed
by all of the others. All except David – God's choice –
whom Jesse didn't think to invite.

We're just as ignorant of God's glorious plans – and
just as much a part of His continuing story! Never
underestimate your place on this planet. God desires
that your life's legacy be linked to birth of the King, too.

*If the grandfather of the grandfather of Jesus had
known what was hidden within him, he would
have stood humble and awe-struck before his soul.*

KAHLIL GIBRAN

Listen to Others

For this reason I remind you to fan into flame the gift of God, which is in you through the laying on of my hands.
2 TIMOTHY 1:6

In Bible class the other day, someone gave an account of going to Joplin on a relief mission after the tornado destroyed a large chunk of the town. He had gone to help people clean up and rebuild their lives during his summer break. As I listened to him describe what the tornado had done to these people's homes and lives, I sat there feeling very petty about how bothered I was by some of the inconveniences I deal with in my life, and how I felt that some of my needs weren't being fulfilled.

Wow, I was thinking totally about myself! That jerked me back into reality and made me leave my pity party. Too many times I let all the obstacles in my life extinguish my flame, making me more of a black hole instead of a shining beacon for Christ.

Sometimes, it takes hearing about others being a good Christian to make me realize that I'm not burning with brotherly love anymore and that I need to be relit.

At times our own light goes out and is rekindled by a spark from another person. Each of us has cause to think with deep gratitude of those who have lighted the flame within us.
ALBERT SCHWEITZER

Scar Tissue

Everyone should be quick to listen,
slow to speak and slow to become angry.
JAMES 1:19

I was angry and frustrated with my son about his unwillingness to help me. I felt betrayed by his lack of gratitude and indifference to all the things I do for him. I knew I had taught him to be better than that. I see him treat others right and have had many proud moments observing those traits, but at that moment I needed his help.

I really lost it. I was yelling and saying things that should have never come into my mind, much less paraded out of my mouth. When I realized I had gone too far, I felt very embarrassed by my outburst. I was very repentant for all the things I said to him in my rage.

We talked twenty minutes or so later. Both of us became emotional, expressed more clearly how we felt, apologized for bad behavior and words that were said. We reemphasized our love for each other. In the future, I will pay more attention to what I say, because harsh words can leave a mark.

People who fly into a rage always make a bad landing.
WILL ROGERS

Love One Another

Don't just pretend to love others. Really love them.
ROMANS 12:9 NLT

Confession time—I love, love, love being "right"—being the one who knows the stupid piece of drivel about which actor played which role in which movie; or which football team won the most Superbowls; or the memory about what really happened (important details like "it was Monday, not Thursday").

I do this with faith, too. And, while Jesus certainly told the woman caught in adultery to "sin no more," "sinners" (in other words, the non-religious) genuinely liked hanging out with Him.

How'd He pull that off? By truly and deeply loving people. Exactly what does this kind of loving look like in regular, everyday life? I don't know. But I'm determined to learn.

No one ever converted to Christianity because they lost the argument.
PHILIP YANCEY

Communicate

My dear brothers and sisters, take note of this:
Everyone should be quick to listen,
slow to speak and slow to become angry.

JAMES 1:19

The best-selling book, *Men are from Mars,*
Women are from Venus won millions over just by the title.

It captures the helpless and frustrating feeling that often accompanies two people of the opposite sex trying to communicate. It is sometimes so difficult, the notion of being from two different planets makes a lot of sense!

Of course, communication takes great care and skill regardless of gender. It breaks down between a father and son, a boss and employee, two brothers, two guys on the golf course – you name it. And when it does, all hell can break loose. St. Francis offered the world inspired insight when he wrote:

> O Divine Master, grant that I may
> not so much seek ... to be understood,
> as to understand.

My, my, what a difference this perspective can make.

I wish people who have trouble communicating
would just shut up.

TOM LEHRER

Be Content

I know how to live on almost nothing or with everything.
I have learned the secret of living in every situation,
whether it is with a full stomach or empty,
with plenty or little.

PHILIPPIANS 4:12 NLT

I'd like to tell you I'm impenetrable to whiney, wimpy seductions like envy or jealousy or self-pity – and I could, too (of course, I'd be lying).

The truth is, these are powerful and stealthy invaders. Unlike the duck's clunky, waddle-based approach to flight, self-pity can soar into our psyches. And, once its hawk-like talons take hold, it can rip your world in half before you shake yourself free.

The apostle Paul talked about this. He said contentment was something he had to learn. It wasn't automatic. It didn't magically take him over the day he became a follower of Christ. It was developed one challenge at a time. That's how it will be for us, too.

I had the blues because I had no shoes until upon the street,
I met a man who had no feet.

DENIS WAITLEY

Take Action

Come into His city with songs of thanksgiving
and into His courtyards with songs of praise.
Thank Him and praise His name.
PSALM 100:4 NCV

Ten folks with leprosy are told by Jesus to go
and show themselves to the priests. As they walked, they
were healed. Presumably, all noticed their healing but
only one – a foreigner – came back to thank Jesus.

Here's a bit of trivia: the man who came back did
a 180 the moment he saw his skin clear up. Another
tidbit? He wasn't guarded in his enthusiasm. Instead, he
fell at Jesus' feet and – with a loud voice – praised Him.

Jesus asks him the obvious question (rhetorically, I'm
guessing): "Where are the other nine?"

That thankful feeling in your heart is merely the
prompter of the action that is supposed to follow. If it
remains a privately cooed upon warm and fuzzy feeling,
you may not be thankful at all. Just very, very satisfied.
It appears Jesus thinks there's a difference. If so, we
should, too.

Silent gratitude isn't much use to anyone.
GLADYS BRONWYN STERN

Choices

*I press on toward the goal to win the prize for
which God has called me heavenward in Christ Jesus.*
PHILIPPIANS 3:14

Obstacles can make the road to your goal
treacherous and send you on one bumpy ride. Mankind
seems determined to focus on the obstacles instead of
focusing on the goals.

I always have twenty-five reasons as to why I can't do
something instead of telling exactly how I can do it. All
those "can'ts" can really build a massive pile-up on the
highway of life and keep me from seeing down the road.
Sure, I'll have some fender-benders on my journey, but as
long as I look only for things that will prevent me from
staying on course, then I'll never see my destination on
the horizon, even if I'm close to arriving there. It could
be just around the bend.

Of course, mapping it out before I begin my travels
helps tremendously. That way I can avoid some of those
obstacles waiting for me and choose a better route. That's
what being a Christian is all about ... choosing the better
route. Maybe I should let Jesus be my GPS.

*Obstacles are those frightful things you see
when you take your eyes off your goal.*
HENRY FORD

Be Content

*Keep your lives free from the love of money
and be content with what you have.*

HEBREWS 13:5

You can look around in almost any home in America and see that most people are not content with what they have. We want more; no, we need more.

At least that's what we try to convince ourselves. I see an ad on TV and almost immediately, "I need that!" comes out of my mouth. "Honey, we need to get a new lawnmower. Don't you think we need a bigger TV? How about picking up another movie when you go to the store?"

I always need something that is newer, bigger, faster, better, shinier, more comfortable, or makes me look slimmer. I never seem to have any problem finding one more thing to buy.

Yet, I don't feel better. I'm not any happier once I have all those things. Usually it's the opposite. I look around and see all the junk I didn't need piling up around me like the reality shows about hoarding. I might not be quite as extreme as some on the show, but it scares me how little it would take to get there. All I know is that it's not very fulfilling.

*People who live the most fulfilling lives are the ones
who are always rejoicing at what they have.*

RICHARD CARLSON

The Clock Is Ticking

Lord, remind me how brief my time on earth will be.
Remind me that my days are numbered —
how fleeting my life is.
PSALM 39:4 NLT

Remember being ten and dreaming about being a teenager? It seemed like it would never arrive. But thirteen came and went and almost instantly you dreamed of turning sixteen and having your driver's license. That came and whooshed right by, too.

As we age, the clock's hands seem to hasten their pace as if they're in a rush to get somewhere, dragging us along. One day we look up and wonder where the years have gone.

A flipside view is the antidote. We can use our days in such a way as to turn that whoosh into a warmth, that feeling of loss into a legacy of love. This, of course, is something we mustn't put off any longer. After all, the clock is ticking.

The future is something which everyone
reaches at the rate of sixty minutes an hour,
whatever he does, whoever he is.
C. S. LEWIS

Living Water

O God, You are my God; earnestly I seek You;
my soul thirsts for You; my flesh faints for You,
as in a dry and weary land where there is no water.
PSALM 63:1 ESV

It was a record-setting heat wave summer and my garden was showing serious signs of struggle. I went out to check on it and, to my horror, saw half of it in full-wilt mode. I raced to the water hose and began dousing them, literally praying I wasn't too late.

I often experience a special connection with God when I'm tending my garden and on this day God's divine whisper went to the center of my soul. Living water – that's what I heard.

I immediately found myself transported into a new level of understanding as I watched the leaves of my cantaloupe, squash and pepper plants slowly regain their vitality. It was like watching a metaphor materialize before me.

Lord, I prayed with a new clarity and passion, give me this living water. Help me to remember this day and hold fast to my own desperate need for Your sustenance.

I need you, like the flower needs the rain,
you know I need you.
RECORDED BY THE BAND, AMERICA

Silence Is Golden

The Lord is in His holy temple;
let all the earth be silent before Him.
HABAKKUK 2:20

Years ago, a friend of mine suggested I go on a fast – a silence fast. No talking for three days. At first, I was offended.

"You're telling me to shut up."

"Well, yes, but not in the way you're thinking."

I'll admit I don't like unsolicited "help" like this but I do try to be open to others' input – even when it's hard to hear.

"Three days?"

"Yep. Force yourself to listen."

I was startled to see how much I miss because of my mouth.

I was amazed, too. I caught myself pondering more, allowing things to develop without my interruptions of what I thought. I listened to nature, to the birds, water bubbling over rocks, the gravel under my feet as I walked. Before it was over, I think I even heard ... God.

I believe in the discipline of silence,
and could talk for hours about it.
GEORGE BERNARD SHAW

Procrastination

The hand of the diligent will rule,
while the slothful will be put to forced labor.
PROVERBS 12:24 ESV

I have serious struggles with procrastination (just ask my publisher). There's something in me that seems bent on sabotaging my own productivity. Why would I want to put things off that I'd feel great about getting done? Wait. This sounds like Paul: What I want to do, I don't do.

I don't usually think Romans seven is about procrastination. It's about our huge, overwhelming sinful nature – right? But couldn't procrastination be as much a part of my sinful nature as, say, lust or greed? Don't they all lead away from the "life to the fullest" God promises? Doesn't procrastination – when fully obeyed – bring about theft, destruction, or even death?

God empowers us to live in power and freedom. Anything that keeps us from that might just be a tool in the hands of our adversary. Be alert. Be vigilant.

The greatest thief this world ever produced is
procrastination, and he is still at large.
HENRY WHEELER SHAW

Be in Prayer

And pray in the Spirit on all occasions
with all kinds of prayers and requests.
EPHESIANS 6:18

When I was young, I thought when you prayed you needed to be on bended knee, hands folded, and eyes closed. Of course, my thoughts on that changed over the years. Yet, I think there are probably many out there who feel that praying to God only happens when you do it intentionally. I now think that God hears many of our prayers even when our lips aren't moving.

Sometimes, when driving down the highway or sitting in the park, my mind goes into deep meditation and peruses what I did that day or how I treated others on my daily journey. Many times I realize that maybe I didn't make the best decisions or represent God in a way that would shine His light into a dark world, yet I know that God knows every thought I have even before it happens.

These thoughts are definitely prayers, as I realize my mistakes and contemplate on how to make amends for anything that didn't live up to Christ's example.

There are thoughts which are prayers. There are
moments when, whatever the posture
of the body, the soul is on its knees.
VICTOR HUGO

Be Thankful

Give thanks to the Lord, for He is good;
His love endures forever.

1 CHRONICLES 16:34

So many times we go through our day never thinking about how many wonderful things we have in our lives. Little things like breathing, seeing the smile of an old man, hearing a baby coo, noticing the blooms of an iris, feeling the warmth of the sun, or enjoying the freedom we have in our country are all blessings in our lives. We're so used to having so many things that we don't recognize how grateful we should be.

In fact, we're usually the opposite, citing all the things we wish we had. Suddenly, I can't get my mom's words out of my mind, telling me countless times not to waste food while children around the world are starving. At the time, all I could think about was hoping she shipped it overseas so I wouldn't have to eat it. Never satisfied instead of being thankful, I wanted something different or more of what I already had. God has given us so much. Realization is the first step, then comes acknowledgment.

God gave you a gift of 86,400 seconds today.
Have you used one to say "thank you?"

WILLIAM A. WARD

Real Love

Charm can mislead and beauty soon fades.
The woman to be admired and praised
is the woman who lives in the Fear-of-God.
<small>PROVERBS 31:30 MSG</small>

In the classic children's book *The Velveteen Rabbit* the shy bunny feels inferior to the modern and mechanical toys in the nursery. "What is real?" he asks the wise Skin Horse. "Does it mean having things that buzz inside you and a stick-out handle?"

"Real isn't about how you are made," he said. "When a child loves you for a long, long time, not just to play with, but really loves you. Then you become real."

"Does it happen all at once, like being wound up?"

"It takes a long time," said the Skin Horse. "Generally, by the time you are real, most of your hair has been loved off, and your eyes drop out and you get loose in the joints and very shabby."

Here's one of the wisest statements ever written: "But these things don't matter at all, because once you are real you can't be ugly, except to people who don't understand."

Guard your heart lest your love for your lover in lingerie lessens your love for your lover.

If love is blind, why is lingerie so popular?
<small>ANONYMOUS</small>

Real Faith

For you are all children of God
through faith in Christ Jesus.
GALATIANS 3:26 NLT

It seems to me, lots of us get confused about exactly what faith is. We often think of it as being more akin to a strongly held hunch than to an entrance into a fixed reality. We approach faith like we approach a swimming pool – toe first to sample the temperature, followed by the dreaded incremental immersion where we slowly lower ourselves underwater one shockingly cold inch at a time, always in control, always able to get back out at any moment.

Faith, as illustrated in the Bible, is rarely like that. It's the desperate woman who pushes through the crowd to touch His prayer tassels that moves Jesus most. "Woman," He tells her with obvious delight, "your faith has healed you!"

Maybe it's time to quit being so "grown-up" about this "faith thing." Maybe it's time to be a child again, to see the pool glistening in the sun, drop the towel and race our friends to be the first in the water – extra kudos to the one who makes the biggest splash!

Feed your faith and your fears will starve to death.
ANONYMOUS

Tender Words

Love one another with brotherly affection.
Outdo one another in showing honor.
ROMANS 12:10 ESV

It wasn't the sort of closing phone call comment you normally hear from your realtor. We had been looking at houses with Kurt when our financial situation suddenly changed and we were going to have to forego a move. I called Kurt to explain.

The conversation took a somber tone as I confessed it was a difficult time for us personally but that we really appreciated all he had done to help us. Kurt listened with great compassion, then, as we were wrapping up the conversation, he said: "I love you." I wasn't ready for that! "Er," I stammered, "I, um, think you're swell, too ... bye." I hung up, bewildered but touched. The phone rang instantly. It was Kurt, embarrassed. "Did I just tell you I loved you?" "Um, yeah." He laughed nervously. "I'm so sorry. Something about our conversation got me confused. I thought I was saying bye to my dad!"

I love that I was given a front row seat to his tender relationship with his father. Kurt's blunder became a blessing to me. And still is. Tender words can do that to a man.

Do not save your loving speeches for your friends
till they are dead: Do not write them on their tombstones,
Speak them rather now instead.
ANNA CUMMINS

It's Not Over

*Elijah came to a broom bush, sat down under it
and prayed that he might die ... All at once an
angel touched him and said, "Get up and eat."*
1 KINGS 19:4-5

I was whining to my wife tonight about how I'm
fifty and have so little to show for all my years on this
earth. What's more, discouraged as I was, the future
looked like a whole lot more of the same. Not my most
shining moment! The good news in all that? It's just a
moment.

With a little bit of perspective or a good night's sleep
or one task done better than expected, those tsunamis
of despair will sink deep into the sand and a promising
sunrise will spread its cheer atop the peaceful water once
again.

It's easy to waste a life looking back in regret or
staring bleakly into the future. It can be addictive, too.
Let me restate the obvious: you're still here. Translation:
it ain't over. The horizontally-challenged lady hasn't
sung. Meaning? There's still stuff for you to do, people
to encourage, burdens to lift, words to speak, vision to
cast, hands to hold, children to inspire, shoulders to hug,
tears to dry, wounds to heal, insights to gain, wisdom to
share, experiences to ... experience. Starting now.

*Here is the test to find whether your mission on
earth is finished. If you're alive, it isn't.*

RICHARD BACH

Life-Saver

Say to those with fearful hearts, "Be strong, do not fear;
your God will come, He will come with vengeance;
with divine retribution He will come to save you."

<small>ISAIAH 35:4</small>

When it rains, it pours. It took many years for me to realize that this saying was talking about more than salt. After several traumatic events in my life, one after another, I was starting to feel a lot like Noah, except for the fact that Noah had built an ark to weather the flood.

The only boat I saw in my future looked an awful lot like the Titanic. Not so sure I was too excited about taking that trip! Can I get a refund on these tickets? Yet somehow I stayed afloat, hanging on to whatever driftwood came my way.

Fortunately, that driftwood was God. He hangs around waiting for whoever chooses to reach out and grab onto the safety He offers. He kept me afloat during teenage tribulations, rocky relationships, stresses of parenting, bad work situations, and family health problems. He even lifts me back up out of the dangerous storms of temptation when I'm willing to hang on for dear life. We're all going to have many sorrows come our way, but no matter what happens, God is there for us.

When sorrows come, they come not
single spies, but in battalions.

<small>WILLIAM SHAKESPEARE</small>

Discipline

*For the Spirit God gave us does not make us timid,
but gives us power, love and self-discipline.*

2 TIMOTHY 1:7

Discipline is a big battle for me. I'm not disciplined enough in my diet. My constant procrastinating on getting things done is definitely a lack of discipline. If I were more disciplined, I'd stick to things a little longer and see a reward for doing so, but so often I give up because I just don't like to do pain. Pain is a four-letter word.

Being disciplined requires consistency, another thing I struggle with. It seems that inconsistency is one of the few constants in my life. Being disciplined means putting in more effort so you can get where you're going.

When I fail to stay the course and put in the hard work, I'm often filled with a regret that eventually eats at me because I know that had I stayed true to what I was aiming for, I could have hit the mark. Maybe even a bull's-eye!

We must all suffer from one of two pains: the pain of discipline or the pain of regret. The difference is discipline weighs ounces while regret weighs tons.

JIM ROHN

Pick Up Your Mat

"Would you like to get well?"
JOHN 5:6 NLT

The man was truly pitiful. The Amplified Bible says he had had a "deep-seated and lingering disorder for thirty-eight years." Deep-seated. Hmm. We don't exactly know what this man's ailment was; some translations simply say he was sick, others use the word incapacitated. His own words confirm the latter.

Thefreedictionary.com defines incapacitated as *deprived of strength or ability*. I think this fits him well. It was also deep-seated and lingering. That's a deadly combination. Injuries – physical or psychological – always seek to become emotionally defining and, once they take root, you better buy a comfy mat to lie on as you're likely to be there for a long, long time.

But a word can save it just as it saved this stuck man lying beside the pool of Bethesda day after day. The word Jesus spoke is called life. The man grabbed hold of that life and, in doing so, ended thirty-eight years of despondency.

"Rise, pick up your mat, and walk." Are these your words today?

Don't wait for a light to appear at the end of the tunnel, stride down there and light the bloody thing yourself.
SARA HENDERSON

Fitting In?

Obviously, I'm not trying to win the approval of people,
but of God. If pleasing people were my goal,
I would not be Christ's servant.

GALATIANS 1:10 NLT

Who likes being the only one who doesn't get the joke? Or the only who came dressed in a pirate costume to the black tie banquet? Or the only Steelers fan in Cowboy Stadium?

It's nice to fit in. We're social creatures, after all. But too much "going along to get along" will gradually get you somewhere you never would've gone.

The walk of faith is a journey lived simultaneously in community and isolation. Spend too much time in either and you'll lose your way.

Whenever you find yourself on the side of the majority,
it is time to pause and reflect.

MARK TWAIN

Perseverance

I have fought the good fight,
I have finished the race,
I have kept the faith.
2 TIMOTHY 4:7

Boy, do I struggle with that! Perseverance is really difficult, especially when your mind is telling you to stop, give it up, let it go. They say, "No pain, no gain," but pain isn't a good time. After all, isn't that what everyone wants … a good time?

Unfortunately, most good times don't lead to anything worthwhile or that lasts much past that initial good time. I remember my Dad telling me that doing something I didn't want to do would build character or make me a better person. It certainly did not seem so at that moment, but eventually I found out what he was talking about.

One time I had to tell the store clerk I had taken some candy I hadn't paid for and had to apologize. That wasn't a good time. It was a hard pill to swallow, for sure; but in the long run it made me a better person.

I've already had many struggles in my life and will have many more to come, but it sure makes it easier if I face them one race at a time.

Perseverance is not a long race;
it is many short races one after another.
WALTER ELLIOTT

Go, Fight, Win

Watch and pray so that you will not fall into temptation.
The spirit is willing, but the flesh is weak.
MATTHEW 26:41

Temptation is so tempting! What is it about being human that so many things tempt us at every turn? That sure smells good. She really looks great! That music sounds so soothing. This cake tastes delicious! See how soft this fabric is.

Temptation affects all our senses. Our senses are constantly bombarded with things that make it hard to resist temptation, but we need to fight back and not give in.

Yep, it's difficult, because we want it so badly that we tend to find a way to justify succumbing. If I buy this flat-screen TV on sale now, I'll save a bundle. One bite won't kill me; I'll start my diet tomorrow. I'll count this lunch as a business expense. Mr. Smith won't ever miss this apple off his tree. There's hundreds, no, thousands of examples I can use here.

Complacency takes over way too often in accepting a lack of resistance to temptation, as well as many other shortcomings. You can't resist temptation if you don't put up some kind of fight. Go, fight, win out over temptation.

What makes resisting temptation difficult for many people is they don't want to discourage it completely.

FRANKLIN P. JONES

Live in Peace

*If possible, as far as it depends on you,
live at peace with everyone.*
ROMANS 12:18

Before Paul's conversion, he was a real up-and-comer among the religious elite. A "Pharisee of Pharisees" (his words). We first meet him self-righteously smiling over the stoning site of Stephen. Later, he hopped on his stallion and rode from town to town, hunting new believers down. Passion? Paul had it.

There's a curious little verse preachers have a lot of fun with. It comes on the heels of Acts 9:29-30 which tells how the converted Paul was whisked off by fellow Christians to Tarsus to keep the Grecian Jews from killing him. It reads simply: "Then the church ... enjoyed a time of peace." The implication is that Paul was still driving the Christians crazy – only this time as an insider!

I'm like that sometimes. I let my own little obsessions – holy as they may occasionally be – drive others to the brink. Jesus never annoyed anyone into righteousness. He spoke truth "for those who have ears to hear." If Christ gave others such space, I certainly should, too.

*Some cause happiness wherever they go;
others whenever they go.*
OSCAR WILDE

Generosity

Whoever is generous to the poor lends to the Lord,
and He will repay him for his deed.
PROVERBS 19:17 ESV

One thing is a constant with money – you never have to convince someone to like it. However, keeping them from loving it, well, that's a horse of a different color! Money translates into power: power of influence, power of prestige, power of personal choice, power of calling the shots. Money winks and whispers, "Trust me." God steps in and says, "Careful."

According to Scripture, we shouldn't love – or hate – money. Money is simply a commodity to be exchanged back and forth. It's when it stops flowing that problems sneak in. We pile it up. We hoard. We lengthen our shopping lists.

The antidote is generosity. When we use money to define ourselves, money always ends up in charge. God calls us to freedom in every area – including our bank accounts.

Money is better than poverty,
if only for financial reasons.
WOODY ALLEN

Living for Others

"The greatest among you will be your servant."
MATTHEW 23:11

History is strung together by grand-visioned people who caught hold of something and refused to let it go until it materialized before them. We admire some of them and, rightfully, loathe others, but we know their names just the same. We study the wake of their lives and, though they're long dead, we still find ourselves influenced by them.

The real question is "why so few?" Out of the billions who've come and gone, as well as those here now, why do most pass away hardly noticed, hardly felt by the bulk of the world? Isn't there enough grandness needed on this planet for each to walk in some? And, by grandness, I'm not suggesting typical heroics like winning a great battle or discovering the cure to a major disease.

The grandness I'm speaking of is simply living your life for someone other than yourself, the kind of grandness that, if it leads to notoriety at all, is intrusive and unsought. Like that of Mother Teresa or Ghandi. Or Jesus.

Want to make your mark on this planet? Spend your life improving the lives of others.

Do not follow where the path may lead.
Go instead where there is no path and leave a trail.
HAROLD R. McALINDON

Think Long-Term

Do nothing out of selfish ambition or vain conceit.
Rather, in humility value others above yourselves.
PHILIPPIANS 2:3-4

I met Elmo when I brought a potential buyer to see his house. "The property line is just over that ridge," he pointed out. "How'd you manage to get the best lot of the bunch?" I asked. Elmo smiled. "I'll bet I pulled three hundred trees up back here – and about that many in the front. Sure makes a difference."

Pointing out twenty-five saplings, evenly spaced along the fence that lined the side of his property, he added, "I got all these planted last week. Twenty more and I'll be finished." I was impressed that this man of 85 years was so hardy but what rocked my world was how invigorated he was to be planting trees he'd never see.

In a culture obsessed with short-cuts to instant success, money and happiness – and, more personally, in a heart as cluttered with self-absorption as mine – I'm thankful to have met a renegade named Elmo: an unheralded General in a revolution of "under-the-radar labors of love" solely for the benefit of a future belonging entirely to someone else.

One generation plants the trees,
another gets the shade.
CHINESE PROVERB

Honest Thoughts

My beloved speaks and says to me:
"Arise, my love, my beautiful one, and come away."
SONG OF SONGS 2:10 ESV

Forgive me, Father, I have sinned. It's been six days since my last devotion. I mean, honestly, odds are, after a gap like that, I wouldn't bother to do another one. And, since I'm being honest, I certainly thought about not doing another one – thought long and hard about it. I mean, nobody's making me do this. I also pondered the possibility that these quiet moments are all for naught and a silly and, ultimately, unimportant "discipline" in "the big scheme of things." I even got mathematical, figuring I'd done enough of them to have "earned" a break. Lastly, I went practical: Odds are, I debated myself, I won't be doing these forever so, realistically, now would be as good of a time to stop as any.

Yet here I am, once again, trying to side up next to You, hoping for a holy insight, starving to feast on Your goodness or, at least, catch a few crumbs from Your table. Oh, just to simply be in Your presence. Thank You. Amen.

It's just You and me here now.
DAVID CROWDER BAND

Consider This

But among you there must not even be a hint
of sexual immorality, or of any kind of impurity,
or of greed, because these are improper for God's holy people.
EPHESIANS 5:3

A hit TV show began with a montage of four different couples peeling each other's clothes off in a mad dash to their beds – or stairs if that's as far as they made it. What's a guy to do? We're worked up enough! But now, 70% of TV programs include sexual content (twice as much as in 1998). George F. Will nailed it when he said, "It is no longer enough to be lusty. One must be a sexual gourmet."

No doubt about it, God created sex for pleasure. But also to give us entrance to a deeply mysterious union. A union too fragile for an "anything's okay if you're married" approach.

Ready for a jolt? If you can't pray while you play, you might be going the wrong way.

What most men desire is a virgin who is a whore.
EDWARD DAHLBERG

Anger

*Do not be quickly provoked in your spirit,
for anger resides in the lap of fools.*
ECCLESIASTES 7:9

Every time I saw that photo in the picture album, I wondered why my brother had his hands clenched and his little red face looking like he was about to explode.

My mom said they would tell him to "show me you're mad," and that's the expression he would make. I always thought that was a cute story, but there's nothing cute about being angry.

Angry words? Now we have a game called, *Angry Birds* that millions of children and adults are spending hours playing. Have we become oblivious to how much harm anger can cause? It's so difficult to have good judgment when you're angry; and sometimes it makes you act irrationally.

I know I've blurted out things or done something that I wanted to make go away by putting everything in reverse. Just push rewind and take it back. That would be great! Speaking without thinking is one of my specialties. Most of us regret showing our anger, but wouldn't it have been better if we had never even felt it in our hearts?

You cannot shake hands with a clenched fist.
INDIRA GANDHI

Peer Pressure

Blessed are those who act justly,
who always do what is right.
PSALM 106:3

Peer pressure can be one of the hardest things to withstand. You want others to like you. You need to be "one of the gang." You don't want to be the odd man out or stick out like a sore thumb.

Peer pressure makes teenagers tattoo their bodies and pierce their tongues. It gets neighbors to buy things they really can't afford to keep up with the Joneses. It convinces young girls that starving their bodies is a good thing because thin is in and everyone wants to look like models. It talks you into breaking the law or getting high because you've got to be cool. It lures you into unscrupulous actions at work to climb that ladder of success, so much so that you're willing to step on whomever necessary to make it to the top.

Yes, it's hard to do the right thing. Going against the flow can be a struggle. I've heard too many teachers ask, "If Billy jumped off a bridge, would you jump, too?" I always thought that was a stupid question. I mean, cheating wasn't anything like jumping off a bridge! Now I can see there are many different types and sizes of bridges in our lives, but the fall is equally dangerous.

Right is right, even if everyone is against it;
and wrong is wrong, even if everyone is for it.
WILLIAM PENN

You Matter

Now to Him who is able to do far more
abundantly than all that we ask or think,
according to the power at work
within us, to Him be the glory.

Ephesians 3:20-21 esv

In his book *The Divine Commodity* author Skye Jethani writes about Vincent Van Gogh's famous painting *Starry Night*. He tells of Van Gogh's disillusionment with what he called, "that God of the Clergymen" while still very much longing to connect with the Creator.

Skye writes, "Like Vincent a century earlier, I fear the contemporary church is losing its ability to inspire."

As a youth pastor, I want our youth to catch a vision for what God has in mind for each one of them, to get stoked about the urgent reality that their life matters.

We see examples of it here and there and when we do, our hearts leap inside us. It may be in hearing someone with a gift for singing. It may be witnessing a spontaneous act of kindness.

This is what it is like to walk with God, to be "in the moment" responding, acting on, obeying, seeing the creative invitations of God. These are not stale repetitions. They are life-changing, holy innovations inspired by God Himself.

God calls us to life, not to routine.

I would sum up my fear about the future in
one word: boring. And that's my one fear:
that everything has happened.

J. G. Ballard

The Little Things

"Do to others whatever you would
like them to do to you. This is the essence
of all that is taught in the law and the prophets."
MATTHEW 7:12 NLT

Ask your average "man-on-the-street" the difference between good and great, average and stellar, adequate and top-notch and you'll likely hear him say, "It's the little things." Occasionally you will come across someone who pays your parking meter when you're out of change, or wash your car after you've had it serviced.

The truth is, this doesn't make someone a stand-out as often as it will cause folks to stand off for fear this person is either starving or psychotic. The reason the summation "it's the little things" is used so often is because most often it is the little things that promote "good" to "great" or elevate "so-so" to "so incredibly awesome." It's that extra deed or word or service.

Small stuff is kingdom business, too. God calls us to light our world by being a good neighbor, treating people right, you know, the "doing unto others" types of thing. Simple stuff, really, and wholly transformational.

The ordinary acts we practice every day at home
are of more importance to the soul than
their simplicity might suggest.
THOMAS MOORE

Baby Steps

Brothers, I do not consider myself yet to have taken hold of it. But one thing I do: Forgetting what is behind and straining toward what is ahead.

Philippians 3:13

One of my family's favorite movies is *What about Bob?* Bill Murray plays a psychiatrist's nightmare. He can hardly muster the courage to get out of bed. The movie starts with Murray's last psychiatrist desperately shoving Bill off onto another psychiatrist. The new psychiatrist gives Bill a copy of his just published self-help book entitled *Baby Steps*. The premise being that we don't accomplish most things all at once but rather in increments – i.e. baby steps.

It's a hilarious movie and, silly as it sounds, it actually offers great advice. Need to lose 40 lbs? Don't expect to drop it overnight. Take baby steps toward it. Say *no* to that dessert. Choose water at your meal instead of a soda. Want to draw closer to God? Baby steps can help there, too.

Don't fall into the deception of thinking you're going to get everything right – you're not! Just keep on keeping on! Do one thing in the right direction. Then another. Then another as if learning to walk again – which, in truth, is what we're always doing.

Sometimes it's slow-going, but there's a knowin' that one day perfect I will be.

Christian camp song from the '70s

No Excuses

*"Just say 'yes' and 'no.' When you manipulate
words to get your own way, you go wrong."*
MATTHEW 5:37

It's easy to promise the moon but impossible to deliver it. Luckily for me, I carry an extra large backpack of excuses.

Sooner or later, others will get my number – that's a fact. The strange thing is how long it takes for me to admit it to myself. It's called denial and denial is definitely not our friend. Denial simply sweeps reality under the rug till the carpet becomes Mt. Everest.

Unfortunately, when we finally get to the point of confronting it, many precious friendships, opportunities and blessings will have been destroyed along the way.

Maybe it's our desire to be liked that leads us to inflate our admiration for something. Maybe it's our desire to be a part of something that makes us commit to things we have little intention of following through. Maybe it's our fear of being rejected?

Stop making excuses and then don't let yourself start making excuses for why you made excuses in the first place. Just dig in and start.

*The best day of your life is the one on which you
decide your life is your own. No apologies or excuses ...
This is the day your life really begins.*
BOB MOAWAD

Friendship

*"There is no greater love than to lay down
one's life for one's friends. You are My
friends if you do what I command."*

JOHN 15:13-14 NLT

As a youth pastor, I often see the role of friendships through the lives of the kids in our group. I "follow" their Facebook conversations and am constantly reminded of how vulnerable friendships leave us.

Here are a few online statuses at the time of this writing:

Every time I trust somebody, they show me why I shouldn't.

I love you. If you need someone to talk to I'm here. I will be no matter what!

If our friendship was a movie the theme song would be, *Hot & Cold.*

Certainly God wants us to be the kind of people who exemplify a truly good friend, but does He likewise want us to be overly dependent on friendships for our sense of self-worth? I have my doubts.

As we grow in God we will, at times, have to reject the painful evaluations of others – and this isn't a teen-only struggle. It's hard as a grown-up, too.

*True friendship is a plant of slow growth, and must
undergo and withstand the shocks of adversity,
before it is entitled to the appellation.*

GEORGE WASHINGTON

Strength from Troubles

We are afflicted in every way, but not crushed;
perplexed, but not driven to despair.

2 CORINTHIANS 4:8 ESV

My wife and I watched a documentary about some true heroes. They thought of themselves as ordinary (something all true heroes tend to do). But had they been like everyone else around them, entire generations of families would not exist today.

These heroes were teachers at a home in France during WWII who risked their lives to love, teach, train, protect and hide numerous orphaned Jewish children from Hitler's horrific hate machine.

We watch a lot of documentaries related to this terrible time in our history. There's something very compelling about this group of sturdy people who survived such prejudice, persecution, evil and cruelty and yet went on to live truly productive and engaged lives. Many are still among us today. The amazing and yet bewildering thing is how many of the survivors speak of the strength they gained from those horrendous times.

Life tests our faith. Setbacks roll out the red carpet hoping we'll walk down it and forever be knocked off-course. Troubles try to wash us away like tsunamis but if we stand, our legs will strengthen enough to support us.

A faith that hasn't been tested can't be trusted.

ADRIAN ROGERS

Thinking of Sin

For the wages of sin is death, but the free gift
of God is eternal life in Christ Jesus our Lord.
ROMANS 6:23 NLT

Comedian Flip Wilson gained nationwide fame during the '70s with his female character "Geraldine."

Geraldine was prissy, sassy and known for giving in to a world of temptations. She'd brag about her escapades and immediately explain her actions away by saying, "The devil made me do it!" It was funny stuff. Of course, good humor has to ring true on some level and her winking at sin is something everyone understands.

There's nothing new about loving sin, but the results of doing so have been painfully clear since the beginning of time.

The main reason we keep giving in rests more on our stubborn grip for self-rule than on the promised pleasures of the indulgence. It's about rejecting God's values in preference to our own. It's about trusting ourselves to know best and distrusting God. Next time you're tempted, think of temptation as a rejection of God's sovereignty and it may help diffuse some of its allure. Like the dieter's motto: A minute on the lips, forever on the hips, sin's motto might well be: a death-embracing diss for a momentary bliss.

The trouble with resisting temptation is it
may never come your way again.
KORMAN'S LAW

Real Humility

Create in me a pure heart, O God,
and renew a steadfast spirit within me.

PSALM 51:10

David was, by most standards, quite the stud. Since his youth, he was heralded as a hero for killing Goliath. As a young man, he married into royalty, which didn't hurt his wallet. He was best friends with a prince. He was a skillful warrior, commander, and leader. He was a musician, songwriter, and poet. He was quite a hit with the ladies. And, if all that wasn't impressive enough, he also lived a life so spiritually passionate that God Himself called him "a man after God's very heart."

It isn't often that a man with this caliber of resume would be such a genuine embodiment of humility. And yet, David was. As amazing as his list of accomplishments was, David knew he was far from perfect and desperately in need of God's mercy, forgiveness and restoration.

Instead of "believing his own press" and making excuses for his sins, he wept, he prayed, he fasted and covered himself with sackcloth and ashes in repentance for his wrongs. In other words, he humbled himself, which, in God's eyes, is the most impressive part of all.

Humility is the foundation of all the other virtues: hence,
in the soul in which this virtue does not exist there cannot
be any other virtue except in mere appearance.

ST. AUGUSTINE

Transitions

Pile your troubles on God's shoulders –
He'll carry your load, He'll help you out.
He'll never let good people topple into ruin.
PSALM 55:22 MSG

Our oldest moved out of the house this summer. We celebrate his growth and all the wonderful things going on in his life but every now and again we feel the sting of that chapter in our lives being over.

Of course, that's how life is supposed to be. Pregnancies bring forth babies who grow into toddlers who grow into kindergarteners and so on. It's a bitter-sweet reality – but mostly sweet.

Just as we walk from one room into another, life is a succession of transitions. How we exit one room determines how we'll enter the next one. We carry that perspective into our next opportunity. If we leave feeling betrayed, we're going to enter guarded. If we leave feeling unappreciated, we're going to enter looking for ample affirmation from the new boss and, in doing so, we set ourselves up for verse two of the same song we just sang.

What we need is a new perspective. God can give us that if we bring it to Him. Once we do, we have to embrace His healing at every wounded level and boldly walk out in His power.

Often when you think you're at the end of something,
you're at the beginning of something else.
FRED ROGERS

Stay Committed

In the same way, husbands ought to love their
wives as they love their own bodies. For a man
who loves his wife actually shows love for himself.

EPHESIANS 5:28 NLT

I was watching a documentary about materialism and was surprised to hear them link it to the breakdown of the family. It immediately rang true. One of the characteristics of a materialistic mindset is discontentment with the "old" and a hunger for the "new."

As a society becomes more materialistic, they exhibit the same casualness with discarding relationships – even the most sacred ones.

We discard things not on the basis of their quality or function or usefulness but solely on the basis that they are, well, "yesterday."

It's a mindset, a cancerous corruption of our convictions that blinds us to better judgment. Completely uninterested in the long-term consequences, we "short-term" ourselves into a stream of quickly fading satisfactions.

We know the foolishness of believing "the grass is greener on the other side" and yet we scrape ourselves trying to climb over. There is no perfect mate (I'm including you, by the way. And me!). Be a radical. Live to bless and honor your wife. Regardless.

Nearly all marriages, even happy ones, are mistakes:
in the sense that almost certainly ... both partners
might be found more suitable mates.

J. R. R. TOLKIEN

Faith Is Action

I could go on and on, but I've run out of time.
There are so many more — Gideon, Barak, Samson,
Jephthah, David, Samuel, the prophets …
Through acts of faith, they toppled kingdoms,
made justice work, took the promises for themselves.
HEBREWS 11:32-34 MSG

Most of us think of the word *faith* as a noun, as in my faith. It's not that this is entirely wrong. It's just that it's often misleading.

Faith, like love, is a verb. It isn't something we can box up or put on a base and display on a shelf. Likewise, faith isn't a surge of intense feeling — like a conviction on steroids — though it sometimes comes on us urgently. Even in that moment, faith isn't the urge — it's what is trying to come out!

Faith is something we can make manifest only by action. Before it gets implemented, it is only an invitation to faith, an on-ramp, a stirring to bring it forth into expression. It sounds like semantics, I know, but, in application, it is worlds apart. Do you know the saying, "Put your money where your mouth is"? That's faith in a nutshell.

Faith isn't faith until you're holding on to it.
ANONYMOUS

Freedom

*"God blesses those who hunger and thirst
for justice, for they will be satisfied."*
MATTHEW 5:6 NLT

A documentary I watched recently said that 1957 was the year with the greatest percentage of people who described themselves as "very happy." In the 50s, only about 33% of homes had a washing machine, 10% had telephones, and the average size home was just less than 1,000 square feet (it's twice that today).

There is no argument that we have more conveniences and access to technological innovations, and yet, according to the PBS documentary *Affluenza*: "In 1995, eighty-six percent of Americans who voluntarily cut back their consumption felt happier as a result."

Surprising? It shouldn't be. The writer of Ecclesiastes noted years ago: "Vanity, vanity, all is vanity – a chasing after the wind!"

Then he concluded with this great, seasoned treasure: "After all has been heard and pondered, this is the sum of life: 'Fear God and keep His commandments, for this is the entire duty of man'." Not only will it set us free from the stranglehold of possessions, it will also set us truly free.

*The real measure of your wealth is how much
you'd be worth if you lost all your money.*
ANONYMOUS

Hope

Why, my soul, are you downcast?
Why so disturbed within me? Put your hope in God,
for I will yet praise Him, my Savior and my God.
PSALM 43:5

In 2007, suicide was the seventh leading cause of death among adult males, and the fifteenth among adult women. That's terrible, you say. And you're right. Why do almost 35,000 people in the United States end their lives each year? The same reason countless millions fall into depression: life is hard. There are ups and there are most definitely downs, and, of course, it's the downs that can take us all the way under, if we let them.

Joseph was familiar with pits – literally. He experienced one setback after another for the bulk of his life and yet something kept him going even when the whole world seemed determined to do him in. It was hope.

I read of a girl who was buried in earthquake rubble for fifteen days and survived. How? She explained: "I knew someone would save me, so I hung on."

Hope enables us to press on when everything seems hopeless. But God!

When you fall into a pit, you either die or get out.
CHINESE PROVERB

The Golden Rule

*Let each of us please his neighbor for his good,
to build him up.*
ROMANS 15:2 ESV

Mary Kay Ash, better known as simply "Mary Kay" – the founder of the worldwide Mary Kay Cosmetics empire, knows a thing or two about connecting with people. One of her stated goals for her life was to "live my life in such a way that when I die, someone can say, she cared." She certainly succeeded.

Her secret turns out to be not so big of a secret at all. It was, in a nutshell, the "golden rule." Treat others like you'd like to be treated. In other words, make them feel important.

Obviously, this continues to be one of the key ways for innumerable sales people to succeed but it was a life principle long before the corporate world turned it into a mantra. It was the primary characteristic of Jesus' life. But, of course, with Jesus, it wasn't a tool to build up His ministry. No, it was simply Jesus expressing the heart of God. There was no sales commission tied to it, no cloaked desire to increase earnings. It was simply Jesus showing the world the Father. We are to do the same.

Pretend that every single person you meet has a sign around his or her neck that says, Make Me Feel Important. Not only will you succeed in sales, you will succeed in life.
MARY KAY ASH

Free to Worship

May the words of my mouth and the
meditation of my heart be pleasing to You,
O Lord, my rock and my redeemer.
PSALM 19:14 NLT

In Nathaniel Philbrick's book, *Mayflower*, he tells the story of the early settlers to North America. I wasn't a stellar student but even I knew it wasn't the easiest of times.

During the first year in Jamestown, 70 of 108 settlers died. The next winter, 440 out of 500. Wait, it gets worse. Between 1619 and 1622, 3,000 of the 3,600 sent over, died. Why did so many risk so much? Philbrick explains "they were willing to endure almost anything, if it meant they could worship as they pleased." Wow. Think about that.

Today, we have churches on virtually every corner, catering to a world of doctrines, denominations, personalities and tastes. We have cowboy churches and homeschooling churches and mission-focused churches and seeker-sensitive churches, and that's just a few! Why so many? The same reason as those adventurous settlers – freedom to worship as we please.

The bigger question is – who does our worship please?

Caged birds accept each other but
flight is what they long for.
TENNESSEE WILLIAMS

Put Others First

"The Son of Man did not come to be served, but to serve, and to give His life as a ransom for many."
MATTHEW 20:28

Blame it on the Greek philosopher Epicurus who, way back around 300 BC, taught that life's highest goal should be to minimize pain and maximize pleasure.

Blame it on TV preachers who constantly insist that our happiness is God's chief obsession. Better yet, blame it on ourselves for making the silly slogan "God wants you to be happy!" into a Messianic mantra.

No doubt, God is the source of all true joy but all too often we turn this message into a mess. God is not a genie, buffet or vending machine and the surest way to feel completely empty is to spend your days pigging out on your pleasures.

The way to real happiness is found not in amassing personal feel-goods but in putting others first.

What was really needed was a fundamental change in our attitude toward life ... it did not really matter what we expected from life, but rather what life expected from us.
VIKTOR E. FRANKL

Fear

The Lord is my light and my salvation –
whom shall I fear? The Lord is the stronghold
of my life – of whom shall I be afraid?

PSALM 27:1

Fear is a fog or – as FDR's generation experienced – a dust bowl of, in Roosevelt's famous words, "nameless, unreasoning, unjustified terror which paralyzes". This is the very energy and vision that we need to turn the seductive cycle around. Worse still, "fear makes come true that which one is afraid of."

If fear is a death-row prison sentence (which it is), embrace God's sovereign "presidential pardon" by doing, well, almost anything fear insists is pointless.

Punch fear's pillow-talk counsel packed with "Why bothers?" and "All is for naught!" grumblings with a powerhouse performance of David's 23rd psalm! That'll sort fear out. And when fear comes back (and it will) give him another round of earth-shattering faith.

The only thing we have to fear is fear itself.
FRANKLIN D. ROOSEVELT

Be an Example

*The words of the reckless pierce like swords,
but the tongue of the wise brings healing.*
PROVERBS 12:18

There are so many things we can do to make the world better if we just allow the glow of God's glory to shine through in our lives. Some of these might just be little things, everyday things, things that might seem so inconsequential to us yet might mean the world to another.

Things we do and things we say are seen by unknowing eyes. Think about how many times words fly ever so trippingly off the tongue, too late to be taken back. There I am thinking, "I sure wish I could take them back."

We touch people's lives every day without even knowing it. Many times these "touches" start a ball rolling that eventually leads to changes, changes we may never see; nevertheless, changes that started from our example, good or bad.

Make sure you're healing lives, instead of opening new wounds.

A good deed is never lost: he who sows courtesy reaps friendship; and he who plants kindness gathers love.
ST. BASIL

"Soul" Food

"If anyone gives even a cup of cold water to one of these little ones who is My disciple, truly I tell you, that person will certainly not lose their reward."

MATTHEW 10:42

How many times do I ask myself if I'm being the kind of Christian that embodies Christ? So many times I feel that, you know, I'm not a "bad" person. I haven't really done any BIG sins, but I'm also not doing actions that scream out, "Hey, I'm a Christian and not ashamed to let anyone else know it!"

Just like there aren't big lies and little white lies, there also aren't big acts of Christian love and little ones.

I think God sees a simple act of kindness given from your heart with as much excitement and pride as with those acts where you really knocked it out of the park.

Going to the fridge and bringing a cold drink to my loving wife, helping an older person with the door at a restaurant, or showing my fellow workers consideration by letting them know what a great job they're doing, are all ordinary acts. These simple acts simply make us better people and mirror Jesus in many ways that touch others' hearts. That's what I call real "soul" food!

The ordinary acts we practice every day at home are of more importance to the soul than their simplicity might suggest.

THOMAS MOORE

Hope

"I know the plans I have for you," declares the Lord,
"plans to prosper you and not to harm you,
plans to give you hope and a future."

JEREMIAH 29:11

Hope. Thank the Lord we have hope. Where would we be without hope? You'd have nothing to look forward to. You'd have no goals to set, nothing to achieve. You'd sit mired in your own desolation, your own foolishness, your own lack of worth. Well, think about it! You'd basically be in your own hell.

The reason God sent His only Son was to give us hope, hope of a better future, hope of an eternal life. Everyone has hope. They might not always see it. It doesn't always just stare you in the face. Many times you have to look for it. Sometimes you have to dig deep for it, but it's there ... for everyone.

When you do find it, it gives you that gold ring to reach for, something to hold onto, because we all need hope to keep going. We're bombarded daily with so many ungodly thoughts and deeds that we HAVE to have hope to replenish our hearts and souls. Hope is that song in your heart that keeps you going. Listen. I can hear it now.

Hope is the thing with feathers
That perches in the soul
And sings the tunes without the words,
And never stops at all.

EMILY DICKINSON

Strong Souls

"Therefore I tell you, do not worry about your life,
what you will eat or drink; or about your body,
what you will wear. Is not life more than food,
and the body more than clothes?"

MATTHEW 6:25

You may not be able to judge a book by its cover, but so many people do just that with others. Most Americans are obsessed with how they look for this reason. We care too much about what others see when they look at us. We spend way too much time trying to "rewrap" the package God made, instead of just taking care of what He gave us. We don't want others to look at us with distaste or pity. That's why we spend hours every week in the gym and eat like birds trying to fulfill an image that our society constantly shoves down our throats.

Why don't we put forth that same effort in strengthening our souls? It's our souls that God cares about. Strong souls don't just happen. Strong souls are built from constant repetition of thinking the right thoughts, having the right heart, acting the right way, being a righteous person. Get the lead out and give me the body of Christ!

Choose rather to be strong of soul than strong of body.

PYTHAGORAS

Failure

Now we pray to God that you will not do anything wrong.
Not that people will see that we have stood
the test but so that you will do what is right
even though we may seem to have failed.

2 CORINTHIANS 13:7

If at first you don't succeed, try and try again. Sound familiar? There are many ways I've heard that same thought over the years, but the message is always that you need to keep plugging away no matter what comes your way. Most everyone fails at something in life. Failure happens. Any time you try something, failure is a possibility, but not an inevitability.

When failure does happen, it's how you handle it that makes a difference. Do you sit there telling yourself that's just the way the cookie crumbles? Or do you pick yourself up, dust yourself off, and start all over again?

Christ had roadblocks before Him at every turn while on earth. People did not believe He was the Messiah. Even after performing many miracles, people still doubted Him. Still, He kept on keeping on. Having faith in your abilities is just as important as faith in God because He made you. He gave you those abilities, and He doesn't make mistakes. If you try, you might fail, but never fail to try.

The greatest glory in living lies not in never failing,
but in rising every time we fall.

NELSON MANDELA

Be Truthful

Truthful lips endure forever,
but a lying tongue lasts only a moment.
PROVERBS 12:19

We want to hear the truth, the whole truth, and nothing but the truth in court, but truthfully speaking, we live in a world where to tell the truth doesn't always seem to be everyone's goal. Instead, we seem to prefer "stretching the truth" to where sometimes it takes on a totally new shape where the original is barely recognizable.

Well, if the truth will set you free, then why do we have such a hard time telling it? Doesn't everybody want to be free? The truth can be a difficult task to accomplish, especially if doing so comes with consequences that aren't very appealing.

It's so much easier to not quite give the whole story or fabricate a new one. And we certainly don't want to use the word "lie". It has such an ugly connotation to it. But if we see it for what it really is, then maybe we wouldn't do it so often.

A half-truth is a whole lie.
YIDDISH PROVERB

Growing

*Whatever you have learned or received or heard from me,
or seen in me – put it into practice.
And the God of peace will be with you.*

PHILIPPIANS 4:9

We all want to grab that gold ring, but few want to do what it takes to be able to do so. Anything that's worth achieving usually takes some extra effort.

In order to win the game, you've got to practice until you reach your potential. You don't just walk onto the field and win the game because you really want to win. Attitude's important, but it is not everything.

Christianity is like that, too. We all want to mature in our Christian life, but you can't just want it. You have to work at it every day because each day that you're striving to be better IS your daily practice. You have to work hard to reach the goal of becoming a mature Christian.

You have to be willing to make sacrifices like you do in sports, give up things so you're totally focused on your goal. Even as a Christian, sometimes you have to take one for the team because the good of the majority outweighs the good of the one or the few.

*It's not the will to win, but the will to prepare
to win that makes the difference.*

PAUL BRYANT

Forgive

Brothers and sisters, I know that I have not yet reached that goal, but there is one thing I always do. Forgetting the past and straining toward what is ahead.
PHILIPPIANS 3:13 NCV

Sometimes a bad memory can be a real blessing. Too many times I go back to the past when I get in a conflict, whether it be with my wife, co-workers, my children, friends, and even with fellow Christians. I need to let the past go and start anew with each situation, but that seems to be one of the few times that I have the memory of an elephant.

This is when I need to follow the lead of the Heavenly Father. I want Him to be able to forgive me for all the sins that I commit, forget all the mistakes I constantly make. Yet, when someone else makes a mistake, especially if it's directed toward me, the first thing I do is drag up the past and make sure that I shove it right in their faces.

But God doesn't do that to me. All I have to do is pray to Him and simply ask for forgiveness, and He gives it to me because Jesus already took care of that debt. Bring on a memory lapse!

One of the keys to happiness is a bad memory.
RITA MAE BROWN

Smile

"In the same way, you should be a light for other people. Live so that they will see the good things you do and will praise your Father in heaven."

MATTHEW 5:16 NCV

I firmly believe that a smile is contagious. It's really difficult to not feel better when you're around someone who is constantly smiling. People always tell my wife that she's got a smile on her face whenever they see her. She's always in an extraordinarily good mood considering she can't walk and spends most of her time in a wheelchair ever since she had a stroke a couple of years ago.

Her smile makes them smile and generally puts everyone in a happy mood. I know I feel better when I see her shining face smiling. It's like a light that is beaming from her soul and making its way out through her eyes and smile.

The light from her happy attitude ignites a light within those around her, brightening everything within her general vicinity. Even when I'm feeling down, it's hard not to feel better, and before I know it, I can feel the corners of my lips start creeping up like an involuntary muscle spasm. Suddenly, I realize I'm smiling, too.

Those who bring sunshine to the lives of others cannot keep it from themselves.

JAMES M. BARRIE

Other Books in the *GodMoments* series

GodMoments for Women

GodMoments for Moms

GodMoments for You